44 Reasons
Your Mixes Suck
A Mixing Engineer's Guide

Amos Clarke

First publication in May 2018. 44 Reasons Your Mixes Suck, Copyright 2018 - All Rights Reserved – Amos P. W. Clarke

ALL RIGHTS RESERVED. No part of this publication may be reproduced or transmitted in any form whatsoever, electronic, or mechanical, including photocopying, recording, or by any informational storage or retrieval system without express written, dated and signed permission from the author.

Amos Clarke

About this book

Welcome and thanks for getting hold of my book. If you're stuck in a mixing rut, then hopefully this book will help you out of it. Even if you're a reasonably experienced engineer, then perhaps you might find a snippet or two of usefulness, or you might have a chuckle at the whacky drawings - yep, they're mine.

As you work through this book, some of the 'reasons' may seem like song-writing problems rather than mixing issues. You may feel comfortable blaming the artist because of their poor composition skills and your resulting lackluster mix.

However, listeners don't care about the reasons *why* your mix sounds below par. You'll never hear a song that starts with a disclaimer from the mix engineer! Mixing engineers are in a precarious position and can get blamed for other peoples' mistakes: musicians who can't play, singers who can't sing, poor songwriting, second-rate production - the list goes on. This invariably means that to maintain our reputation, we have to act as the gatekeepers; the last bastion of defense for the song. Therefore, it's our duty as a mixing engineer to act professionally and raise any issues that may affect the quality of the finished song mix, that way, everybody wins.

Carrying out this 'quality assurance' part of mixing means that we need the skills to identify the problems, like listening for disharmony or pointing out poor song format.

However, many of the problems associated with a second-rate sounding mix are much more fundamental than those just mentioned. They result from poor mixing decisions, bad habits, and a lack of understanding and experience.

Hopefully, this book will help. I've tried my best to bring you 44 of the main reasons that make a mix sound amateur. I hope you find it useful.

Note: Any time a specific plugin or manufacturer is mentioned, it's purely as an example or suggestion. The author is in no way, affiliated to or intending to promote a product or company.

Free Stuff for my Readers

Please join my reader group to get my FREE eBook,
EQing for Gold
It contains the essential equalisation techniques you need to know to clean out the mud, define your midrange, and make your tops sing.

You also find out about upcoming book releases and other free stuff that will help your mixing and production.

Please visit:
www.44reasonsyourmixessuck.weebly.com

Amos Clarke

1. It's too damn loud!

Thanks to the loudness war, so many amateur mixing engineers think that a pro mix must be a loud mix. So, they cheerfully load up their favourite limiter plugin onto the master buss and drive the level so hard that the final mix file looks like a brick. The problem is that doing this destroys the transients, which are the very elements that make a mix sound punchy. A 'slammed' mix has a limited dynamic range which can raise the noise floor and can cause distortion in the mix. This flawed approach makes a final mix almost impossible to master.

Solution:

Ditch the limiter on the master buss. Ensure your peaks NEVER hit 0 dBFS on the digital meter. Aim for an average loudness level of -14 to -12 dB.

2. It sounds too harsh

Harshness in the mix is generally caused by unwanted distortion and excessive frequency content in the 2 - 4 kHz range. It's very common when using cheap, harsh-sounding condenser microphones and cheap digital converters. The issue gets worse when a multitrack session has many tracks exhibiting harshness. The big problem with harshness in a mix is that our ears are naturally fine-tuned to this zone of the frequency spectrum, with too much causing listener fatigue.

Solution:

When recording, use the best quality microphones and interface that you can get your hands on. When mixing, watch your spectrum analyzer and apply subtle EQ reductions in the 2 - 4 kHz region on any tracks that need it. Ensure that any EQ applied to other instruments in this 'harsh' zone is done with extreme care.

3. Unbalanced levels

Balance is the term used for even-ness. If a mix sounds balanced, then all of the musical elements have a relatively even volume level in the mix. It's normal for some levels to be raised in the mix if you want to highlight a musical element, like a lead solo guitar. Amateur mixes often exhibit poor balancing, and a poorly balanced mix is an absolute tell-tale sign that your mix ain't pro!

Solution:

Learning the art of mix balancing takes time, and an excellent way to train your ear is to listen to the mix balancing in your favourite songs. If you're mixing a project, then find a similar sounding professional mix that you can use as a reference. So, park your reference mix on a track in your DAW and refer to it regularly during while you mix. Another tip to help your level balancing is to monitor your mix at a very low volume level while focusing on the mid-range elements. It's much easier to hear when a musical element is dropping out, or popping out, of the mix.

4. Too much reverb

Back in the 80s, lots of reverb was cool. Now it can sound dated. Excessive reverb can also make your mix sound washy and result in a less punchy mix. Probably, a more accurate view is that with modern music, the use of reverb is much more genre specific.

Solution:

Use reverb with care; apply it for a reason. For instance, use low levels to add a little space around a drum kit or lead vocal. Use targeted reverb to make a snare and kick drum sound better in the mix. Try using spacious or long reverb settings to place an element way back in the mix soundstage or to emphasise a lead vocal artfully.

5. It's clipping

We're not talking about hair-cuts! Digital clipping can sound nasty, and there's little excuse for your tracks to clip in this modern age with the high dynamic ranges available in consumer-level recording and mixing systems.

Solution:

Turn stuff down, seriously! When mixing, check your recorded audio clips for clipping as well as your overall track, group, and master buss volumes. If the recordings are clipped, then you may need to re-record or repair them with specialist repair software, like Izotope RX6. If your track outputs are clipping, then check that your plugins are not creating unnecessary boosts and lower their output levels. Reduce the overall level so the highest peaks are at -5 dBFS on your peak meter. Check your group busses, sends and returns, and your master buss and reduce the level.

6. Too bright

Overly bright mixes are another noob mistake where the engineer over-emphasises high frequencies in an attempt to add clarity to the mix or elements within the mix. The problem is that these extreme highs throw the mix out of balance relative to the midrange and bass regions of the mix and this can be fatiguing for listeners.

Solution:

Let's discuss two solutions to this. Firstly, whenever you want to add clarity to a musical element, try removing/reducing the frequencies of competing instruments. Any further clarity you need to achieve with your focus-element will likely require only a small emphasis. For instance, if you find that your lead vocal is lacking clarity because it's fighting with a wall of distorted electric guitars, send the guitars to a group and gently roll off the high frequencies with a low-pass filter while listening to the mix. The vocal should become more intelligible. A small (up to 3 dB) EQ boost to the vocal in the 5 - 10 kHz region should give you the clarity you want without resorting to significant, ear-fatiguing increases. The second solution is to regularly refer to a reference song that's similar to your mix. Listen carefully to the blend and emphasis of frequencies in the low, mid, and high range and try and emulate these in your mix.

7. Poor panning

The problem with panning mix elements to unexpected positions in the mix panorama is that it sounds strange and often uncomfortable for the listener. Poor panning choices can make a mix sound lop-sided, increase masking problems, and more. Listen to early popular recordings to hear entire drum kits panned to one side, giving a strange perspective on the band setup. As vinyl recording technology evolved, low-frequency instruments were panned to the middle to avoid the phonograph needle jumping out of the record groove. Years of similar panning styles on radio hits have created invisible panning standards. So much so, that strange panning decisions in modern mixes can seem strange to the average listener.

Solution:

If you want to create a strange sounding mix then by all means, screw around with weird pan positions. But if you're aiming for commercial quality releases then follow what the pros are doing. Here's a guide to get you started on a typical rock song:

Middle pan: bass, lead vocals, lead guitar/keyboard, kick drum, snare drum, secondary rhythm guitars/keyboards, sound fx, samples.
Hard left/right pan: primary rhythm guitars.
Mid left/right pan: backing vocals, keyboards, sound fx, samples.

Note: for more ideas, research the LCR pan method.

Amos Clarke

8. The mix doesn't translate

You worked on your mix for hours in your studio, and it sounded great. Then you played it on your home stereo, and something was wrong; the low end seemed wimpy. So you went back to the studio and remixed it. Then you loaded the mix onto your cell phone, listened with your earbuds, and it had improved, but now it was too bright. Then you played the mix in the car, and it was different again. Back in the studio, you swapped out your regular mixing headphones for a different pair. The mix balance has changed! Finally, you tried a set of prosumer studio monitors, and again, the mix has changed. What's going on? Why does your mix sound different on different systems? But most importantly, how can you get your mix to translate across all listening systems?

Solution:

The above experience is not uncommon when you're new to mixing, so here are a few pointers to alleviate your frustrations:

1. Your mixes will always sound different across the myriad of listening devices. Some headphones accentuate the bass, while small speakers usually lack bass and so it goes on.

2. Avoid mixing on headphones since they don't translate panning in the same way that stereo studio monitors do so.

3. Get the best studio monitors you can afford and treat your listening space. Wall treatment can alleviate resonant frequencies that cause you to make incorrect EQing decisions when you mix.

4. Always use reference songs when you mix. It's the perfect way to help you get a translatable mix since you can compare aspects of your mix with the reference as you work.

9. Drums sound wimpy

For rock, pop, dance and other modern styles of commercial music, the drums are THE essential rhythm element that must be emphasised to transmit the energy required for a successful production. Wimpy, soft-sounding drums just won't cut it. For some genres, like jazz, folk, or alternative music, soft-sounding drums are perfect because they're not required to be a feature. Listen to a reference track for guidance, if you're not sure about how hard your drums should be hitting.

Solution:

There's not enough space in this book to delve into the intricacies of how to get drums to slam and pop, but here are some essential tips that you can go away and research:

1. Mult (duplicate) your snare and kick drum tracks for more volume.

2. Use samples to beef up your snare and kick.

3. Gate your kick, snare, and toms for a clean, punchy sound.

4. Don't clip your drums to make them louder. If you need more drum volume, turn everything else down in the mix.

5. Roll off the lows in your drum overheads to define the kick drum.

6. Accentuate the transient on one of your snare drums to bring it to life in the mix.

10. Not enough low end

A mix can sound thin and pathetic if you don't have enough low-frequency information. Some engineers deliberately reduce the low end slightly since doing so allows the mix to be louder (the low frequencies take up a lot of headroom). But who cares how loud the mix is when it sounds thin from lack of those essential low frequencies. Low frequencies add grunt and thickness to the mix so don't let your mix leave home without them!

Solution:

A typical mix often only has a few elements providing the low end: a kick drum and bass. The mid-range contains the bulk of all the instrumentation in a typical mix. To get an even, overall balance in the mix you need to exaggerate the low elements to get them into balance. Judging the low end can be tough if you don't have a sub speaker and a well-tuned room. To help with this, use a spectrum analyser and your chosen reference song.

11. Not enough high end

Oops! Now your mix sounds dull, like somebody draped curtains over your speakers. Flat sounding recordings sound boring because they lack the high-frequency detail that you would naturally expect to hear from the instruments playing in the song. Sometimes the dullness is due to the way you've been messing around with the mix. It can also be a result of poor recording techniques and poor instrument quality. For example, if the bass player and guitarists are using old strings, their dullness will come through in the recording. Drummers that don't reskin their drums before recording cause the same problem.

Solution:

When recording, players should re-string and re-skin their instruments beforehand. During mix processing, pay careful attention to the high-frequency elements by applying EQ carefully and checking against your reference song.

12. Poor song format

The format of a song is the arrangement of sections, like verses, choruses, and middle-8s, etc. A poorly formatted song can be tedious and, at worst, unlistenable. If your song has five verses before it gets to the chorus, then it's unlikely to hold the listeners' attention. Similarly, if your song is an endless, repetitive loop of verses and choruses, it's likely to be a complete bore.

Solution:

Use a proven song format that works. For instance, a typical commercial pop hit will have this format:
Intro>verse>chorus>verse>chorus>bridge>chorus/outro
With a little research, you'll discover the currently popular formats and the subtle differences that different genres introduce; a commercial rock song will often have a guitar solo replace the bridge or have a solo and a bridge.
But keep this in mind: the chorus is the highlight of the song so don't wait too long to get your audience there.

13. Terrible song

Mixing a terrible song is tough, especially if you're not the composer! It doesn't matter how outstanding your mixing skills are; if the songwriting sucks there's not much you can do because nobody will enjoy the result. Ever heard of the term, 'making a silk purse from a sow's ear'? Or there's the less savoury version, 'polishing a t@#d.'

Solution:

1. Ditch the song and move on to something else.
2. Re-write the song.
3. Do some production work before you start mixing. Consider re-recording parts, removing offending elements, adding samples, recording new parts, and using mixing tricks (like heavy compression, delay-based effects, and multi-effect plugins).

14. Weak lead element

Every song needs a lead element to retain the listener's attention. Lead elements are most commonly a lead vocal, a hooky instrumental melody, or something very catchy (like a rapping vocal). Sure, your song can start with a funky groove from the rhythm section, but at some point (and hopefully not too far away) it needs to introduce something melodic, or catchy that provides the central focus, or lead, for the song. If your song has a steady groove but doesn't go anywhere, it can sound like a backing track. Even worse perhaps, if the song has a weak lead vocal or poorly performed instrumental solo, it will seem very amateurish.

Solution:

Firstly, be sure that you know what the lead elements are throughout your song. It could be a hooky synth melody in the intro, the lead vocal, and a synth solo. Next, ensure these elements are performed well and emphasised throughout the song. You can strengthen the lead even more by emphasising instrumental riffs in the gaps between lead vocal phrases. As an example, check out Emotional Rescue by the Rolling Stones; the first vocal line is immediately followed by a bass/keyboard riff, which is then followed by the lead vocal, and the cycle is repeated. This method of 'fills' is a powerful way to add momentum and energy to any song mix.

15. Excessive distortion

Hey, your song is distorting! There is good distortion and bad distortion. The good kind is deliberate, musical distortion that you want, like your distorted electric guitars or from exciters that you apply to musical elements to give them a bit of wholesome dirt. The bad kind of distortion is the stuff that screams, 'amateur!' It's often caused by incorrect gain structure, like an excessive level on tracks and groups. It can also be produced when you clip your converters during recording, drive your preamps too hard, or distort your mics due to an excessive sound pressure level. Another common reason for distortion in the mix is due to excessive compression and limiting, or excessive equalisation boosts. Whatever the reason, unmusical distortion just sounds plain bad!

Solution:

If the distortion is inherent in the recording, then there is little you can do to fix it since distortion artifacts can affect much of the frequency bandwidth. However, distorted waveforms sometimes occupy a limited band of the overall frequency range. In this situation, you might achieve a fix by using equalisation - HPFs, LPFs, or parametric bell curves - to de-emphasise these zones. On the other hand, if the distortion is happening due to mixing levels then the solution is simple: lower your levels! Bring your track faders down. Check your group faders and master buss and turn them down. Be wary of 'hot' recordings distorting your plugins and fix it by adding a gain plugin at the beginning of your plugin chain.

16. Microphone phasing

Microphone phasing problems can occur in recordings whenever two or more microphones are used simultaneously. Typical situations are when recording with multiple mic's on drum kits; two mics on an acoustic guitar, two mics on a guitar amp, combining a bass D.I. and mic, and any other stereo recording. The resulting sound can be a 'phasy,' modulating sound character that sounds strange, affects the level, and reduces mono compatibility of the mix. Another symptom can be a loss of tone and punch, like when combining a bass D.I. and the mic'd bass amp signal.

Solution:

Phasing issues should be avoided during recording by using careful microphone positioning. Checking for phasing problems is a crucial step in the editing process before mixing. You can quickly do this by soloing the tracks involved, then switching your monitoring from stereo to mono, back and forwards, to see if the tone changes. If unwanted tonal changes are occurring, you can often fix it by moving the position of one of the clips so that the transient peaks are aligned in both clips. Alternatively, you can use a delay-compensation plugin on one track and make fine adjustments until the desired tone is achieved. Sometimes a simple solution is to mute one of the tracks; this could work with the bass D.I./mic problem or a two-mic setup on an acoustic guitar. Fixing phasing issues in the mix can be extremely difficult in multi-instrument setups. For example, time aligning out-of-phase audio clips on multi-mic'd drum kit can be problematic since bringing one drum into phase may put other drums out.

17. Drums not played in time

If there's one thing that *really* stands out in a song, it's a drummer with terrible timing. And it's a compounding problem because the other performers will struggle to keep time with the drummer's chaotic time-keeping. If you're mixing other peoples' recordings, then you either need to fix these timing issues or ignore them. But remember, a poorly-played performance mixed by you will never be great for your reputation.

Solution:

If you record and mix your music, then you've got an opportunity to re-record out-of-time drumming, and it's highly recommended to do so. However, if you're mixing other peoples' music, it's often not convenient to get the drummer back in for another session. The good news is that you can improve the drum timing with some deft editing. Firstly, it's much easier to splice and realign drum hits to your DAW's tempo grid if the drummer recorded to a click track. When editing, it's essential to splice and move ALL of the drum tracks when you adjust timing inconsistencies; ignoring this, can cause phasing on other tracks. You could still make timing improvements by comparing the out-of-time section with the immediately adjacent section even if the drums weren't recorded to a click track. Many DAWs will allow you to see an underlying clip when dragging another clip over the top.

18. Poor clip editing

It's common in any mixing session to splice your audio clips and move them around: drum track clips get cut and pulled into time, vocal phrases get adjusted in time, bass notes are aligned with the kick drum, and so on. If you neglect to do your fades and cross-fades where you splice your clips, you can get nasty clicking sounds at the splice points. Multiply this by lots of tracks, and you've lots of unwanted clicks and sounds that start or finish abruptly and unnaturally.

Solution:

One of your jobs as a mixing engineer is to methodically go through and clean up all tracks before you start mixing. And when you're cutting audio clips, you need to create very short fade-ins and fade-outs at the cut points. You also need to apply cross-fades when two clips overlap. Doing this avoids the unwanted clicks and abrupt starting and stopping of musical elements in the mix.

19. Bumps, clicks, and thumps

One of the hallmarks of a professional sounding mix is the absence of unwanted noise. Bumps, clicks, rumbles, thumps, distortion, clipping, coughs, clanks, buzzing, hum, bleed; it's unmusical, and it's unwanted. The problem gets worse when you consider the cumulative noise of many tracks in the mix and the use of compression, which raises the noise level. This unwanted noise is created in so many ways, from hum in your power supply, to fret clanks from a poorly played bass guitar. You need to be looking for them and removing them from the tracks.

Solution:

It's essential to go through every track in your mixing session, check it for unwanted noise, and remove it. A simple high-pass-filter is an effective way to remove very low-frequency rumble. However, for mid-range and high-frequency artifacts, you'll need an audio editor or repair software that can remove the noise without affecting the integrity of the recorded material. Izotope's RX6 or Acon Digital's Acoustica, are both excellent solutions.

20. Excessive low end

Excessive low-frequency content can cause a finished mix to sound rumbly while affecting the clarity of low-end elements like kick drum and bass. Furthermore, excessive low-frequency energy in the mix can use up a lot of headroom, causing mix-buss compressors to trigger in an unmusical way and reducing the ability to get a loud mix without pumping. These low frequencies commonly occur in most microphone recordings; from drum overheads and acoustic guitars to vocals and keyboards. For example, the lows from a group of distorted electric guitars can cause frequency masking and a lack of clarity with the electric bass.

Solution:

Low-frequency content can be successfully removed using high-pass filtering (HPF). It's good practice to add a HPF as the first plugin on every track and get into the habit of tuning your filter for each track. This is done by soloing the track and slowly raising the filter cut-off frequency until you can hear it affecting the sound, then backing it off slightly.

21. Excessive vocal sibilance

Everyone's heard it in a mix; the overly sibilant vocal where every 'ess' sound is exaggerated. It's uncomfortable and fatiguing to listen to and should be fixed if you want your song to sound professional. The problem often originates from either a poor-quality microphone or excessive use of high-frequency EQ. Cheap microphones often have an artificial presence boost which increases the volume of esses and is a common problem with amateur recordings and mixes.

Solution:

For the recording process, it's essential to use a good quality microphone that is suited to the singer's voice, since these usually don't have the presence boost associated with the cheaper mics. If you're mixing a song and you're stuck with the over-sibilant vocal recording, use a de-esser plugin to tame the esses. Try and avoid merely applying an EQ-cut to the sibilant frequency region as this will tend to create dullness in the vocal parts where no sibilance is occurring.

22. Nasty vocal resonances

Some singers have a nasty resonance that can drill your ears and become uncomfortable for the listener. Often, the problem occurs with female singers who are singing hard in the frequency range of 2 - 5 kHz. The problem is that the resonance can sound exaggerated relative to the rest of their range, often causing a problem with the compressor, where it activates due to the level of the resonating frequency.

Solution:

Here are three solutions to this problem. Firstly, you can use a de-esser and tune it to the resonance zone to reduce the resonances when they occur. Another similar approach is to use a dynamic equaliser, which you can also tune to the desired frequency range. Both of these options automatically enable you to reduce the offending resonances only when they happen. The third and most accurate way to solve the problem is by using volume level automation; you merely draw a volume curve to reduce the volume precisely to the desired level.

23. Poor vocal clarity

The lead vocal rules! Well, at least it should rule in most modern songs. If your listeners can't hear the vocal clearly in the mix, it can just be another example of an amateur production. Sure, some genres, like Metal, have the vocal deliberately buried in the mix. But if you're mixing country, pop, or mainstream rock genres, then your vocal needs clarity. A classic problem with bedroom mix engineers is that vocal articulation varies throughout the song. Sure, you can raise the overall vocal level, but that can then put the vocal out of balance with the rest of the mix.

Solution:

The way to get really clear sounding vocals in a mix without resorting to a significant overall level boost is by using volume level automation. The best way to do this is by adding a simple gain plugin directly before your channel fader and then applying the volume level automation to the gain plugin. Doing this means that even after automating, you can still make overall track level adjustments irrespective of the automation. When automating the level, listen for the moments when the vocal loses clarity - it might only be for one word or even half a word - and automate a small boost. Often just a few dB are all that is required. This method is far more precise than merely relying on a compressor. In fact, often the combination of a compressor and level automation is the perfect solution to get ultimate vocal clarity in the mix.

24. Over-compression

If your mix sounds like the life and soul has been sucked out of it, the chances are that you're overdoing it with compression. A key reason for this is because compression, especially with fast attack times, can significantly reduce the transient (the initial peak) of a recorded sound. And it's the transients that are responsible for adding the punch and snap to your recordings. A typical example is when over-compression reduces the transients in a snare drum track, leaving the snare dull and lifeless, and unable to punch through the mix. This same problem can negatively affect the punch of the entire mix when mix-buss compressors are poorly set. And of course, if you're abusing compressors on the tracks, groups, and mix-buss, then it's a compounding adverse effect on the mix.

Solution:

Firstly, you need to understand the how and why of using compressors. Don't just throw them on every track because that's what the big boys do. You need to know what you're trying to achieve and then select the right compressor and use the correct settings. For example, if you want to add some general leveling to a vocal track, it's good to start with an opto compressor in the style of the LA2A or LA3A. These have a soft-knee compression curve that applies gradual compression relative to the signal level. On the mix-buss, it's essential to preserve the transients to maintain the punch, so an attack time of 30 - 50 ms can give enough time for those snare hits, etc. to pass through before the compressor starts to clamp down. Lastly, with any compression, keep your eye on the gain reduction that you're achieving; anything up to about 3 dB usually provides reasonably transparent compression. Higher levels of GR make the compression more noticeable.

25. Poor performances

There's no doubt that a great song absolutely relies on a great performance. It doesn't matter how fantastic your mix sounds; if the artists can't play and can't sing, then nobody will care about how big, wide, and punchy your mix sounds. Poor performances include the inability to perform in time, wrong notes/chords played, and singers that can't sing in tune. Often, the problem is due to player inexperience, but other times it's due to substance abuse, lack of practise, and player ego. When you're trying hard to build your reputation as a mix engineer, it's wise to limit your involvement in third-rate projects that may be released with your name on them.

Solution:

If the band poorly performs an entire song, the most practical solution is this: don't mix it! However, that's not always great if you're lending a helping hand to a young band or artist. A more rewarding solution for all involved would be to convince the group to rehearse the song and re-record it. This idea of rehearsal before recording is relatively common at a professional level; the mix engineer/producer records the practise sessions, with the recordings being reviewed and performances being tweaked, until the band is 'record-ready.' Sometimes a mix can be rescued if the poor playing is limited to one member, or to only one section of the song. For instance, if it's only the bass player who can't keep time, then some splice-and-nudge might fix poor time-keeping. Similarly, if wrong notes are played, then you can often find the correct note elsewhere in the song and swap it with the offending one. Finally, you need to use your professional judgment about whether a recording is salvageable, mixable, and worth putting your name on.

44 Reasons Your Mixes Suck

26. The mix is too narrow

Some amateur mixes have a very 'mono' sound, resulting in a boring, one-dimensional mix. It's most often noticeable when the mix has many elements since they lack the separation and distinction that could be achieved by taking full advantage of the available stereo panoramic-sound stage. Poor panning choice can exaggerate frequency-masking, causing the mix to sound dull and again, lacking separation and clarity between the elements.

Solution:

Pan your elements with deliberate intention. Try and avoid the mistake of chaotically panning stuff into available 'holes' in the panorama; it just makes a mess. Consider panning elements so that they create balance and width. For example, pan your even equal numbers of electric guitars hard left and right, then pan keyboards to the middle or halfway between centre and hard L/R. Try panning backing vocals in pairs, 50% left and 50% right. To accentuate stereo width, pan instruments with noticeable high-frequency content out wide; your ear is much more sensitive to the pan position of high-frequency elements than low-frequency elements. Lastly, try panning elements based on their frequency range, in other words, avoid panning similar sounding instruments to the same position because they can mask each other.

27. Wrong tempo, poor pace

Have you ever done a mix and put it out for feedback, only to hear that the song seems too hurried or too slow? Perhaps the singer is struggling to keep up, or the entire song seems to drag, creating a dull vibe. Tempo is a critical aspect of any song because it affects the 'pace' of the song. Ideally, you want to avoid being in the position where many hours have been funneled into the recording process only to be left with a mix that that may never sound great due to poor pre-production.

Solution:

If a song's tempo seems too fast, there are ways to manipulate the song's pace so that you can give the perception of a reduced tempo without the headache of time stretching everything or re-recording the song. To fully comprehend this, you need to understand that 'pace' is different from 'tempo.' Where tempo is the beats-per-minute, the pace is driven by the busy-ness of the performances. For instance, the same tempo song can have more pace if many lyrics are sung quickly. The same song with a slower paced vocal delivery gives the perception of less momentum, and therefore, a slower pace. In essence, less busy the performances result in a slower apparent song pace. With that in mind, you can slow the perceived pace by simplifying busy performances, such as simplified bass lines, reducing the number of words to sing or reduce the drummer's hi-hat from 16ths to 8ths. Conversely, you can give more pace to a song that seems to drag by doing the opposite. Try this subtle production technique on your next mix production.

28. Instruments are out of time

If there's one thing that really screams, 'amateur,' it's a mix where the band can't play in time. Not your fault? Maybe; maybe not. This is a problem that appears in degrees, as in, it's either minor timing issues that can be edited back into time or a major assault of poor time-keeping that may be beyond editing. If it's the second one, then you've got your work cut out for you, and it may be better to re-record the song.

Solution:

Majorly lousy time-keeping across most instruments = re-record or abandon the song; it's not worth the endless sweat and teeth-grinding. And it's not worth damaging your rep by putting out poor quality mixes. Minor editing issues can often be fixed without too much difficulty. As mentioned elsewhere, timing edits are usually easily fixed by splicing and shifting musical notes, vocal words, and drum hits back into time. A word of warning though; if you're editing drum timing, splice and move all of the clips in the drum track.

29. Elements are blurred

Something's wrong! Your kick and snare drum hits have a soft, phasing sound when the mix is playing. The vocal track that you duplicated has the simile effect. When you play the individual clips without fx, they sound great. It's killing the vibe and punch of the entire mix.

Solution:

Incorrect delay-compensation within your DAW software could cause the issue you're experiencing. It becomes apparent when two tracks with the same sound playback with a very slight delay, producing a phasing-like sound, being particularly evident between duplicated tracks with percussive sounds. For example, a snare track and drum overhead track with poor delay-compensation can affect the snare sound. The problem is due to the small time delays created by the different plugins applied to each track and the DAW software incorrectly processing these delays. When your DAWs delay-compensation is working correctly, it calculates these time differences and re-aligns the playback time of each track accordingly. Some plugins cause a problem by incorrectly reporting their time delay or not reporting it at all, to the DAW software. The solution is to check your DAW settings to ensure that plugin delay-compensation is active. And if you're having trouble with a particular plugin, try re-installing it or use a different plugin.

30. Excessive pitch correction

Vocal pitch correction is commonly used in professional mixes. Doing it right means doing it tastefully. If you adjust every sung word to be pitch perfect, it will likely sound unrealistic and too perfect. Some vocalists rely on their pitchiness to maintain their fame and character; pitch-shifting Bob Dylan to be note-perfect would be a disaster. Excessive pitch correction on a vocal demonstrates a lack of finesse from the engineer.

Solution:

Pitch correction must be done with care. To do so requires the engineer to listen carefully and apply pitch correction only to those notes that 'feel' wrong. Because of this, pitch-correct can be a bit of a 'black art.' A useful tip is to focus on held notes since their longer duration makes the lousy pitch more obvious. Another approach is to apply a correction to the notes on the 2 and the 4 of the bar. When pitch-correction is executed well, it should be transparent. In other words, you shouldn't be able to hear any artifacts. Cheap plugins can cause warbles, clicks, and weird resonances, so part of the solution to being successful is to use top quality vocal pitching applications, such as Melodyne and Autotune.

31. The singer is out of tune

You've got a problem! You've started working on the mix, and it hit you immediately: the singer can't sing in tune! This is another one of those situations where nobody will care how good your mix sounds because they'll be distracted by a diabolical vocal performance. Most mix engineers are aware that pitch correction software can usually fix the problem. However, abysmal pitching by a singer is often difficult to fix convincingly, even with the best software. Another common problem with amateur mixes is when the singer is just a little bit off pitch throughout the entire song. The untrained ear of the inexperienced engineer doesn't notice the problem and forges ahead, completing the mix. The more discerning listening audience will find such a song to be irritating and unpleasant. And it's unlikely that a mix like this would be considered seriously by a record company or radio programme director.

Solution:

Inferior singing performances on a recording are best fixed by careful rehearsal and re-recording. It's not fun for the mix engineer to tell the singer that they suck, but the good news is that if the problem is addressed with care and respect, the singer can improve measurably. A helpful approach is to sit down with the singer and listen to the performance with the lyric sheet in hand, highlighting the errors, and giving the singer absolute clarity and the opportunity to work on the weak areas. Sometimes it works to change some of the lyrics, revise the phrasing, and even the melody, in an attempt to make the words a better fit for the vocalist.

Amos Clarke

32. Instruments out of tune

Nothing kills the vibe of a song like when one or more instruments are out of tune. As a mix engineer, it's essential to go through each track in your mix and ensure that the instruments are in tune. There are many reasons why an instrument can be out of tune. A common reason that stringed instruments go out of tune is due to players not tuning up before a recording. It's not good enough to only tune up once at the beginning of a session. Players need to tune up between takes since other factors can cause a stringed instrument to go out of tune. For example, brand new strings put on during a recording session tend to stretch and go out of tune since they take time to 'bed in.' Another common tuning problem results when players fret the strings too hard, a problem that can be caused by recording-anxiety or bad habit. A third reason can be due to poor intonation, where the instrument is in and out of tune at different parts of the fretboard - challenging to fix in the mix.

Solution:

Make sure your stringed-instrument players tune up before every take - no exceptions. It's easier if they have a tuner in the signal chain or a clip-on tuner. To avoid intonation problems, ensure that all instruments are set up professionally and restrung before coming to the studio. Before the recording, get the guitars out of their cases and allow them to acclimatise to the temperature and humidity of the studio. Lastly, do your best to create a relaxed atmosphere to help avoid the 'death grip' when playing. Clearly, these are recording issues, so why does the mix engineer need to know all of this stuff? These days, the songwriter, recording engineer, and mixer are often the same person. Even if you're working in a professional environment and only doing the mixing, it's vital to be able to identify performance problems so that you can advise and suggest solutions to the client.

Amos Clarke

33. Cluttered instrumentation

Too many instruments playing at once sounds like a mess. It's the equivalent of listening to an argument. It's tiresome to listen to, and it shows a lack of production and arranging skills, and therefore, screams, 'amateur.' The problem often results from too many melodic mid-range instruments vying for the limelight. Because our ears are sensitive to both mid-range and melodic sounds, engineers need to avoid competing elements in this area.

Solution:

For simple and useful results, it's best to aim for one melodic mid-range element occurring at any one time. With a suitable arrangement, you can get away with two (check out Audioslave, Like A Stone) simultaneous melodies, but any more can lead to a confusing-sounding song because the listener struggles to focus on one element.

34. Singing out of range

Hearing a singer who is singing out of their natural range can sound odd and rather pathetic. In such cases, it's common for the singer to have a problem pitching correctly. Additionally, their vocal tone can seem weak, and with males, they can suddenly start singing in falsetto part way through a phrase. Generally, it's a clear sign that the song is in the wrong key for the singer, or, the singer is the wrong person to sing that song. If this problem is not addressed in the finished mix, it's a clear indication of a second-rate production.

Solution:

If the singer is singing out of their range, then one of two things must change: either the key of the song must change, or the song needs a new singer. The easiest and kindest approach is to alter the key and re-record the song. The critical thing is to avoid the song production getting to the mix stage with this problem. Again, a poor-sounding mix with your name on it is not great for your reputation.

35. Too perfect

The advent of digital audio means that engineers can now apply precision pitch and timing correction to all musical elements. While this allows excellent editing capability, excessive pitch-correcting can easily result in an unnatural sounding performance. While a little pitch and timing adjustment here and there is inevitable on most mixes, a heavy-handed adjustment is a perfect way to suck the life and soul out of your song. The more you correct stuff, the more mechanical it sounds. If you want the mix to sound like humans played it, you must allow slight imperfections in pitch and timing. For instance, a jazz band rhythm section may achieve a wonderfully lazy groove by the drummer adding a little swing into the way he plays the ride, while the bass player may purposely play 'lazy' on the time. An engineer who decides to lock the timing of bass and drums onto a grid can all but destroy such a beautiful, artful groove.

Solution:

A seasoned engineer knows what to adjust and what to leave alone. He/she avoids excessive adjustment because of how quickly the groove can be destroyed. One method for fine-tuning drum timing without killing the feel is to find a bar or two that you feel exemplifies the perfect vibe. Analyse this, looking at how much deviation there is off the beat, and then make adjustments to the rest of the drum track based on this acceptable deviation. And for the rest of the band, ease up a little on your editing. Stop editing pitch and time just because you can. When adjusting the timing on other instruments, aim to get the bass reasonably well locked in with the drums, particularly on the 1 and 3 of the bar, but again, use a light touch and avoid screwing up the band's vibe. By all means, fix those wrong instrument notes but be careful when editing expressive performances, such as guitar or saxophone solos, and adjust pitch and timing conservatively.

36. Excessive fx

Being heavy-handed with your fx is a sure way to distract listeners from the actual song. Often, it's the delay-based fx that cause the problem, with over-cooked reverbs, choruses, phasers, and delays diminishing the clarity and causing blurring of instrumentation as note repetition ride over the top of each other. Drum hits can lose their snap, vocals can lose clarity, and elements can be pushed back in the soundstage, to name but a few of the problems. But it's not only limited to delay-based effects; overdoing distortion effects can soften transients and reduce definition, mainly when applied to many tracks. One of the most significant problems with being heavy-handed with your fx, is that it can upset the balance of your mix. For instance, too much of a phaser can cause significant level increases in particular frequency ranges and dips in others, while excessive stereo chorusing can expand the stereo width of an element, affecting clarity and mono-compatibility.

Solution:

A great cook will add spice to a dish to enhance the flavour, not to change it entirely. Similarly, fx are meant to improve a song, not distract the listener. Occasionally, a song may rely on a heavily applied effect to enhance a hook or give the song a unique sonic blueprint. However, most of the time, fx are like adding spice to your dish. So whatever fx you apply, choose them tastefully and use them carefully.

37. There's no hook!

So...your fans listened to your song, and they said it was boring. What do they know, right? Then you sent it to a music industry contact for feedback, and they said, 'there's no hook!' The upshot is that your song mix is missing a crucial element; a song without a hook is like a birthday without a party. To miss the hook is to miss an essential ingredient. Lastly, don't blame the artist when you publish a mix without a hook. Consider it as your professional responsibility to advise the artist early on if their song is missing this crucial element.

Solution:

A hook is a musical element that grabs the listener's ear. Most folks expect the hook to be part of the chorus, but it doesn't have to be, and you don't have to limit yourself to just one hook in a song. However, if a song doesn't have a hook, it should be identified early on in the mixing process and discussed with the artist. Sometimes, you can find a musical phrase already in the mix and emphasise this to become the hook. Other times it may have to be added to the recording. Don't be fooled into thinking it should always be melodic. A hook can work equally well as a sung or rapped phrase, a unique sound effect or sample, or a hip little drum fill. Check out the hooky rap phrase, 'not many, if any,' in the song, Not Many, by Scribe. Chris Rea's, On the Beach, is a classic example of instant gratification with the song's iconic guitar lead at the intro. Listen to Johan Strauss's, The Blue Danube Waltz, with its melodic hook created by a combination of instruments.

38. Waiting for the chorus

Decades of popular music on the airwaves have conditioned listener expectations. And one of those expectations is that a song gets to the chorus without mucking around. Nobody wants to wait for two minutes or three verses into the song before the party starts. Most of the time it's just boring! And with the vast number of radio stations and online streaming services available, the competition makes it tough keep a listener listening to your song.

Solution:

Very often, you'll find radio hits getting to the chorus within 30 - 45 seconds. Another common formatting approach is to get to later choruses quicker and repeat them more often. This approach saturates the listener with the hook near the end. See the following example:
Intro > verse 1 > chorus 1> intro > half verse 2 > chorus 2 > bridge > chorus/solo > chorus outro.

If the chorus is a long time coming, it's your professional duty to raise the flag and discuss it with the artist before you start mixing. Often, a little shuffling around of the song structure is all that is needed to get the structure right, and this should be done before mixing starts.

39. The missing chorus

Oh, no! Your song has no chorus. Nobody cares how good your mix because the song doesn't go anywhere. But maybe the song does have a chorus, yet poor songwriting has it sitting impotently and unnoticed in the song structure.

Solution:

Every modern song needs a chorus; it's what everybody is waiting for. Sometimes, if the song has a weak chorus, a bit of effort is often required for the mixing engineer to get the spotlight on it and make it something special. This can involve double-tracking instrumentation, adding backing vocals, or simply using automation to lift the volume level of the entire chorus section by a couple of dB. The one exception where it's OK not to have a chorus is when you follow a different song format. Take Burt Bacharach's, I'll Never Fall in Love Again, sung by Dionne Warwicke. This song doesn't have a chorus, but it does have a hook. The song format is AABABA, where 'A' is a turn-around that encompasses the hook and 'B' is the middle-8. This structure is different from the modern format of ABABCB, where 'A' is the verse, 'B' is the chorus, and 'C' is the middle-8.

40. Cheap sounds

Poor sounding samples and instrumental sounds are a dead giveaway of an amateur production. The saxophone solo played on that cheap consumer keyboard just doesn't cut it, just like that thin sounding bass guitar or fake 'picked acoustic guitar' patch. Cheap-sounding keyboard instruments are the worst culprits. Not only can the tone be bad but playing them on a keyboard can sound unrealistic. For example, a pentatonic scale is natural to play on a guitar but not so natural on a keyboard. Of course, if you're not the artist and you end up having to mix a song with cheap sounding instruments, you've got your work cut out for you.

Solution:

If you want to get your mix sounding great, you've got to start with the best quality sounds you can get. There are fantastic sample libraries, keyboards, and software capable of creating great sounds but some investment is usually required. And let's not forget that ol' chestnut of recording the real instrument. However, sometimes, as the mix engineer, you have to make the most of what you've got. While you may not be able to rescue a cheap sounding song, you may be able to agree with the artist to replace vital musical elements, such as instrumental solos and drums.

41. Low bit depth

Your mix is noisy. There's a kind of hiss you can hear running through the entire song. You checked the individual raw tracks, and they sound OK, but when you listen to the mix, the problem is there. And the problem is worse when you get to quiet passages where there is only vocals and guitar playing in the mix. You also noticed that tracks, where you applied a lot of compression, are noisy as well. Is something wrong with your compressor plugins? What's happening? You're using pretty good gear. Why isn't your mix clean and quiet like the pros?

Solution:

The likely reason for your problem is due to recording at low bit depth settings (16 bit and less) and further compounded by recording levels that are set too low. Unfortunately, the problem gets worse when heavy compression is applied to those noisy tracks because it raises the floor level considerably. When you play back many tracks that have this problem, the combined effect becomes noticeable. The solution? Record at 24-bit depth and 44.1 kHz sample rate as a minimum. Furthermore, learn proper gain-staging so that your recording levels are set correctly. For example, aim for maximum recording level peaks of -10 dbFS on your digital meter.

42. Excessive equalisation

Let's face it, when you've got a suite of fantastic equaliser plugins, it's hard not to tweak the EQ on everything; it's so much fun! And while you're having fun being dazzled by fancy GUIs and convincing yourself to make a whole bunch of unnecessary extra adjustments, you're screwing up your mix! Excessive equalisation is one of the number-one rookie moves that's a guaranteed mix-wrecker. The main reason is that it messes with the tonality of the recorded material, and in worst cases, can create nasty resonances in the mix.

Solution:

Firstly, you've got to train yourself out of the compulsion to tweak unnecessarily. Begin the equalisation on your mix by applying low and high pass filters to everything. This approach can hugely add clarity to the mix without screwing up the beautiful tones that the recording engineer tried so hard to achieve. Start by rolling off the unnecessary low frequencies on every track. For example, on your electric guitars, try removing everything below 125 Hz and hear how this adds clarity to the bass guitar. Move on to applying roll-offs to the high frequencies, listening carefully as you work. Apply your roll-offs both in isolation and with the entire mix running. After completing your HPF/LPF roll-offs, listen for the problem areas in each track and aim primarily for EQ reductions, rather than boosts. Muddy frequencies occur around 200 - 300 Hz. Boxy frequencies happen around 400 - 500 Hz. Harshness lives in the 2.5 kHz to 3.5 kHz. Focusing on cleaning up these three areas will take you another big step toward mix clarity. Finally, apply gently boosts where clarity is needed, or you want to accentuate an element. Finally, use your ears, not your eyes, and work with gently subtlety.

43. Harmonic clashes

One of the tough things about being a good engineer is that you need a musical ear if you want to ensure your mixes sound musically correct. It's not enough to have a gorgeous thumping low end and a beautifully articulate midrange if the band is playing the wrong notes and chords. What's worse, is if you cheerfully finish the mix without even noticing!

Solution:

If you're one of those engineers (and there are many of us out there) whose musical talents are limited, you risk putting out mixes with harmonic clashes. For instance, if the bassist is playing riffs in a minor key while the guitarist is playing major chords, you're in trouble. Or if the vocalist sings the odd note in the wrong scale, it can just sound plain wrong. The real challenge is that often these harmonic clashes only occur momentarily, so they're difficult to notice. Another challenge for the uninitiated is the harmonic clashes that can creep into the mix when multiple instruments are playing. For example, it gets tricky with a piano and guitar both comping chords, combined with a sax player and a busy bassist. Even the best musicians make mistakes, and a mix engineer who can identify these issues can be a real asset to any musical production. If your artistic skills are limited, then work with a producer or somebody with a musical ear who can check the harmonic relationship.

44. Wrong key

Having the song in the wrong key can cause some problems: some obvious and some subtle. An obvious sign is when the vocalist is struggling to sing in the correct pitch at the extreme high and low notes in the song. Other times, the singer may be able to hit those high and low notes, but the voice sounds weak or strained: not good. And because vocals are often the critical element in many songs, it sounds second-rate when they are audibly struggling in the mix. A subtle problem that can occur with a wrongly pitched song is that it may screw up the vibe. Generally speaking, as the song's pitch gets higher, the music tends to sound happier. The inverse applies to the key getting lower, where it tends to give a darker, less happy sound. Many songs tend to have their key chosen based on the original instrument used, which is why guitar-based songs are so often written in the keys of E, G, and so on; because they're easy to play!

Solution:

Make sure that the song's key suits the song vibe and the lead singer's range. If you're the songwriter and you're aiming for a sad or angry vibe, in addition to writing it in a minor key, you could check how it sounds played at least one or two semitones above and below your original key. Even a semitone change can make a noticeable difference. Similarly, for that lighter, happier character, try raising the key. Another practical solution is to ensure that instrumentation is played in a higher or lower range within the assigned key. Playing a lower inversion of a chord, again, gives a more somber tone much like chords played in the higher range sound more cheerful. If you're composing or recording comedy and you want to get really happy, use smaller, higher pitched instruments like ukuleles and banjos. Mixing engineers can add immense value to their work by being able to advise their clients about composition and production concepts that will improve their songs.

Free Stuff for my Readers

Please join my reader group to get my FREE eBook,
EQing for Gold
It contains the essential equalisation techniques you need to know to clean out the mud, define your midrange, and make your tops sing.

You also find out about upcoming book releases and other free stuff that will help your mixing and production.

**Please visit:
www.44reasonsyourmixessuck.weebly.com**

Other books by Amos Clarke
Available on Amazon in print and Kindle

Macro-Mixing for the Small Recording Studio
Produce better mixes, faster than ever using simple techniques that actually work

Macro-Mixing for The Small Recording Studio is intended for beginner and intermediate mixing engineers who want to find new ways to massively improve their workflow and the quality of their studio mixes. The book is packed with techniques, examples, guides, and tips to help you create a 'breakthrough' with your mixing. The author includes anecdotes from his own experience working with bands and a range of mixing projects.

Click here to purchase on Amazon in print or Kindle format

56 Mix Tips for the Small Recording Studio
Practical techniques to take your mixes to the next level
AMAZON TOP SELLER

Create magic in your mixes. Flip to any page, read the technique, and

apply it. It's really that simple! 56 Mix Tips gets straight into the business of giving you tried and proven mixing tips that actually work. And there's plenty to keep you busy, covering: compression, equalization, panning, parallel compression, transient manipulation, harmonic distortion, delay-based effects, and so much more. Includes a link to a free online drum processing video tutorial.

Click here to purchase on Amazon in print or Kindle format

Amos Clarke

Song Arrangement for the Small Recording Studio
Practical techniques to take your songs to the next level

Song Arrangement for the Small Recording Studio explores professional techniques for crafting great sounding music productions that will keep your listeners wanting more. Transform your productions by manipulating Builds, Transitions, Hooks, Groove, Pace, Masking, Lead elements (and much more) in your songs. This book compares many of its techniques to popular radio hits so that you can 'see' them in action.

Click here to purchase on Amazon in print or Kindle format

36 Song Arrangement Tips for the Small Recording Studio
Practical arrangement techniques to take your songs to the next level

36 Song Arrangement Tips for the Small Recording Studio is the perfect compilation of song arrangement tips and techniques that will help you create great music productions. This book has similar content to the author's other book, Song Arrangement for the Small Recording Studio, but is formatted into an easy-to-read, tips-based reference (with brand new techniques) that is a perfect studio companion for the songwriter, producer, and mixing engineer. Includes links to free online material.

Click here to purchase on Amazon in print or Kindle format

Made in the USA
San Bernardino, CA
06 December 2019